YOUNG ADULTS

TO

WACKRONYMS™

BY ALAN KATZ AND PETE FORNATALE

AVON BOOKS ◆ NEW YORK

VISIT OUR WEBSITE AT http://AvonBooks.com

WACKRONYMS™ is an original publication of Avon Books. This work has never before appeared in book form.

AVON BOOKS
A division of The Hearst Corporation
1350 Avenue of the Americas, New York, New York 10019

Copyright ©1996 by Alan Katz and Pete Fornatale
Wackronyms™ is a trademark of Alan Katz and Pete Fornatale
Interior design by Elizabeth Van Itallie
Published by arrangement with the authors
ISBN: 0-380-78536-6

Library of Congress Cataloging in Publication Data:
Katz, Alan
Wackronyms / Alan Katz and Pete Fornatale
p. cm.
1. Acronyms—Humor. I. Fornatale, Peter. II. Title.
PN6231.A25K38 1996   96-1065
818'.5402—dc20   CIP

First Avon Books Trade Printing: September 1996

Avon Trademark Reg. U.S. Pat. Off. and in Other Countries, Marca Registrada, Hecho en U.S.A. Printed in the U.S.A.
CW 10 9 8 7 6 5 4 3 2 1

WHAT'S A WACKRONYM ™?

Well, you may know that SCUBA is an "acronym" for Self-Contained Underwater Breathing Apparatus. Or that SNAFU stands for Situation Normal, All Fouled Up. Or that NATO is actually an abbreviated way of communicating North Atlantic Treaty Organization.

Acronyms are shorter, less clumsy ways to remember important expressions.

Now, what if we considered the names of everything we have, everything we do, and everyone we know as an acronym—a shortened version of a longer statement? That would be more than an acronym. It would be…

A WACKRONYM™.

From personal habits, to favorite stars, popular products and more, we've given many of today's hottest subjects the WACKRONYM treatment. After laughing your way through these, feel free to create WACKRONYMS of your own…from your name, or those of your friends and family members.

Good luck!

Alan (A Literary Amazement! Novel!) &
Peter (Please Examine The Evidence Rationally.)

1

"WHO'S WHO?" WACKRONYMS

PEE-WEE HERMAN

PULLING EXTENDED ELEMENT.
WHACKING EXTENDED ELEMENT.
HE EVEN REMEMBERS MASTURBATING
AS NEWBORN.

JAY LENO

JAW'S A YARD LONG. EMMY'S
NEW OWNER.

REGIS

REALLY ENVIES GIFFORD.
INTERESTING? SOMEWHAT.

DONALD TRUMP

DOLLAR OBSESSION NECESSITATES
ARRANGING LECHEROUS DEALS.
TAKES REFUGE UNDER MARLA'S
PANTS.

SUSAN POWTER

SHUT UP! STUPIDLY ADDRESSES
NUTRITION, PREYS ON WOMEN THAT
EAT RAVENOUSLY.

HoWARD STERN

HE'S OFTEN WEIRD AND REALLY DIRTY. SLEAZY TALK ENRAGES REVERENDS, NUNS.

JERRY LEWIS

JERKY ENTERTAINER. REALLY RAUCOUS. YELLS "LADY!" EVERYBODY WANTS IT STOPPED.

DONAHUE

DOLTS **O**N **N**ATIONAL **A**IR**W**AVES **H**AD **U**N**L**I**M**I**T**ED **E**X**P**OSURE.

JOHN TESH

JAWBONE OVERSIZED. HIP? NOT! TUNES EXCRUCIATING. SELLECA'S HUSBAND.

BARNEY

BANAL AND REPULSIVE. NOT
EDUCATING YOUNGSTERS.

ELViS PRESLEY

ENTERTAINED LAS VEGAS iN
SEVENTIES. PRiSCiLLA'S ROMEO
ENGORGED, SLEPT LiTTLE,
EXPiRED YOUNG.

PAVAROTTI

PIZZA AND VEAL AND RAVIOLI.
OPERA'S TWO-TON IMPRESARIO.

DON IMUS

DEEJAY'S OUTRAGEOUSLY NEWSWORTHY INTERVIEWS MOCK UNDERACHIEVING SENATORS.

WAYNE NEWTON

WORKS ALL YEAR. NONSTOP
ENTERTAINER NOT ESPECIALLY
WELCOME TOURING OUTSIDE NEVADA.

CHER

CHECK HER EXTENSIVE RECONSTRUCTION.

OPRAH

OLD **P**ANTS **R**ESEMBLE **A**IRPLANE HANGAR.

DAVID LETTERMAN

DRIVING'S ATROCIOUS. VEHICLE'S
IMPOUNDED DAILY. LIST
ENNUMERATING TOP TEN'S EDGY,
RUDE. MAYBE ABC NEXT?

GERALDO

**GUESTS EXPLOITED REGULARLY.
AUDIENCES LOVE DEMEANING OTHERS.**

PAUL McCARTNEY

PEOPLE APPLAUDED UNTIL LENNON MADE CRITICAL COMMENTS ABOUT ROTTEN TALENT. NOTABLE EXCEPTION: "YESTERDAY."

TOM ARNOLD

TATTOOS OF MOM AND ROSEANNE NOW
OBVIOUSLY LOOK DREADFUL.

ROSEANNE

ROTUND, OBNOXIOUS SLOB EVIDENTLY ATTRACTS NIELSENS, NEUROTICS, ECCENTRICS.

JESSICA HAHN

JESUS EVEN SAYS SHE ISN'T
CHRISTIAN ANYMORE. HOOTERS ARE
HUMONGOUS NOW.

NEWT GINGRICH

NORTH, EAST, WEST, THIS GUY IS NO GOOD. REPUBLICANS IDOLIZE CONSERVATIVE HOGWASH.

MICHAEL JORDAN

MARKETING IS CLEARLY HIS
ABSOLUTE ENDURING LEGACY.
JUNIORS OBEY RELIGIOUSLY, DON
ANYTHING NIKE.

ORSON WELLES

OUTRAGEOUS RADIO SHOW OFFENDED NATION. WOULDN'T EVEN LET LAWYERS EXAMINE SCRIPT.

GEORGE BUSH

GOT ELECTED ON REAGAN'S GROSS EXAGGERATIONS. BUT UNDERDOG STOPPED HIM.

MADONNA

MUSICIAN? ACTOR? DANCER? OR NUT? NAKED, ANYWAY.

BURT REYNOLDS

BIG, UGLY, RIDICULOUS TOUPEE.
REPORTEDLY EASYGOING, YET NEVER
OVERCAME LONI'S DIVORCE
SETTLEMENT.

BRANDO

BOLD ROMANTIC ACTOR
NOW DRAMATICALLY OVERWEIGHT.

JOAN CRAWFORD

JUMPY OLD ACTRESS. NARCISSISTIC.
CHRISTINA REPEATEDLY
ATTACKED WITH FASHION OBJECT
RETAINING DRESSES.

ANNA NiCOLe SMiTH

A NAUGHTY NAKED AMAZON.
NONSTOP iNDUSTRIAL CLEAVAGE.
OLD LOVER EXPiRED.
SO MONEY iS THE HOOK.

RICKI LAKE

REGULARLY INTERVIEWS CREEPY
KIDS, INSANELY LUSTFUL
ASTHMATICS, KOOKS, ETC.

WILLARD SCOTT

WEATHERMAN IS LACKLUSTER LAUGHMAKER. ACTS REALLY DUMB. STILL CAPTIVATES OCTOGENARIANS. THAT'S TODAY.

HiDEO NOMO

HE'S INCREDIBLE! DEFINITELY EXPECT
ONSLAUGHT NOW OF MORE ORIENTALS.

ANN LANDERS

ANNOYING NEWSPAPER NAG'S
LOUSY ADVICE NEVER DISPLAYS
EMPATHY. RETIRE SOON.

JULIA CHILD

Jovial, upbeat. Listen in and cook hippo intestines, legumes. Delicious!

MARTHA STEWART

MISS ASTOUNDINGLY RICH TACKLES HIGHBROW ASSIGNMENTS, SPURRING TOTAL ENVY. WHAT A ROTTEN THING.

MICHAEL JACKSON

METAMORPHOSIS IS COMPLETE.
HE'S AN ECCENTRIC LEGEND.
JUST ASKING: CAN KIDS STAY
OVERNIGHT? NEVER!

TONYA HARDING

TOOK OUT NANCY—YEOWCH! AMERICAN
HOPEFUL ACHIEVED REAL DRAMA.
INCIDENTALLY, NO GOLD.

ADAM & EVE

APPLE DIDN'T APPEAR MURDEROUS.
&
EVERYONE VACATED EDEN.

LEE IACOCCA

LOOK EVERYONE! EMINENT INDIVIDUAL ADVISED CONSUMERS, OFFERING CRAPPY CHRYSLER AUTOMOBILES.

PINTO

PASSENGER IS NEEDLESSLY TORCHED.
OUCH!

FUJi

FiLM USUALLY JUDGED iNFERiOR.

PEPSI

PHOSPHOROUS-ENRICHED POP
SABOTAGES INTESTINES.

POLAROID

PICTURES OFTEN LOUSY AND REALLY OVEREXPOSED. INSTANT DISAPPOINTMENT.

SPAM

SPOILED PROCESSED AMPHIBIAN MEAT.

REEBOK

RIPOFF. EARLIER EVERYONE BOUGHT ONLY KEDS.

SKIPPY

SOME KIDS INGEST PEANUT PASTE.
YUCK!

Bic

BURST IN CHINOS.

CLUB MED

CONJUGAL LOSERS UNITE. BEACH
MAKES EVERYONE DEPRESSED.

AVIS

AMERICAN VEHICLES INFREQUENTLY START.

QVC

QUIRKY VIDEO CRAPOLA.

LYSOL

LOOK, YOU STINK OPPRESSIVELY. LEAVE!

KMART

KEEP ME AWAY. REAL TRASH.

US AiR

UNSAFE SHUTTLE AGAIN IN RIVER.

MCi

MANY CONVERSATIONS INAUDIBLE.

PREPARATION H

PAINFUL RUMP? ELIMINATE PROBLEM
AND RELIEVE A TUSHY INSTANTLY.
OTHERS NOT HELPFUL.

NATIONAL ENQUIRER

NEWSPAPER AVOIDS TRUTH. INSIDE
OBSERVATIONS NASTY, ALL LIES.
EVERY NEWSWORTHY QUOTE
UNSUBSTANTIATED. INTERVIEWS
RARELY EXPRESS REALITY.

COORS

COLORADO'S OBSESSION. OBJECT?
REMAIN SMASHED.

COKE

CAFFEINE OVERDOSE KIDS ENJOY.

SONY

SHREWD ORIENTALS NET YEN.

BMW

BELIEVE MY WEALTH.

FREEDENT

FOAM RUBBER ENJOYMENT.
ELDERLY DELIGHTED. EQUIVALENT?
NIBBLING TEFLON.

McDONALD'S

MEAT'S CRAP. DRIVE OUT NEEDING A LEGITIMATE DINNER SANDWICH.

TACO BELL

TASTY AND CHEAP OILY BEEF.
EVERYONE LOVES LARD.

MTv

MiNDS TURN VAPiD.

ESPN

EXTREME SPORTS? PURE NONSENSE!

LIFETIME

LADIES-IMPRESSIVE FEMALE
ENTERTAINMENT. TUNE IN. MEN
EXCLUDED.

C-SPAN

CONFLICTS. STUPEFYING POLITICS.
AVOID NETWORK.

SALEM

SMOKE A LOT? EXPECT MALIGNANCY.

EDSEL

EVERYONE DRIVES SOMEONE ELSE'S LEMON.

VISA

VANISHING INCOME, SAVINGS ANNIHILATED.

DRAMAMINE

DAMN ROCKING AROUND MAKES A MAN ILL. NAUSEA EXPECTED.

MGM

MORE GARBAGE MOVIES.

SCOPE

SMELLS CAN OVERPOWER.
PLEASE EXPECTORATE.

BINACA

BREATH IS NASTY. ALSO CHECK ARMPITS.

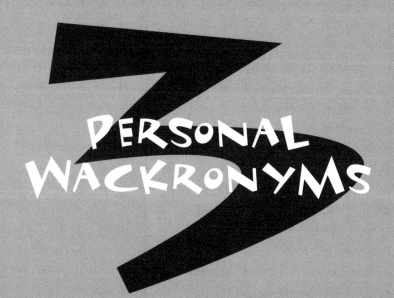

3
PERSONAL
WACKRONYMS

FART

FRESH AIR RUINED. THANKS.

TOILET

TANK OF ILL LIQUID,
ELIMINATED TURDS.

DIAPER

DOODY IN A PORTABLE ELASTIC RECEPTACLE.

EJACULATE

EXTREMELY JUICY ACT.
CONDOM USUALLY LIMITS A
TREMENDOUS EXPRESSION.

MASTURBATE

MAN. ALONE. STROKES.
TOUCHES. UNDULATES. RUBS. BEATS
AND TRIUMPHS. ENCORE!

PENIS

PRIZED EQUIPMENT.
NOOKIE INCREASES SIZE.

DIARRHEA

Doody In Ass Really Rushing.
Hurry, Evacuate Area!

SNOT

SOMETHING NOT OVERLY TASTY.

HiCCUPS

Hi, i CAN'T CHAT UNTIL PROBLEM SUBSIDES.

VIRGIN

VERY INNOCENT, RESPECTABLE GIRL
(GUY). INTERCOURSE? NEVER.

BARF

BURP AND REGURGITATE FOOD.

LUST

LARGELY UNFULFILLED SEXUAL TENSION.

TONGUE

THIS ORGAN'S NO GOOD UNLESS EXTENDED.

FOREPLAY

FRUSTRATING OBLIGATORY ROMANTIC EXPERIENCE. PARTS LONGING, ACHING, YEARNING.

VIEWER'S CHOICE
WACKRONYMS

BAYWATCH

BABES ALL YOUNG. WOEFUL ACTING THAT CLEAVAGE HELPS.

NYPD BLUE

NAKED YOUNG POLICEMEN,
DETECTIVES' BREASTS, LEGS.
UNDERCOVER ESCAPADES.

TAXi

TAKE A XANAX, iGNATOWSKI.

CHICAGO HOPE

CHAOTIC **H**OSPITAL **I**NVOLVING **C**LASSY **A**CTORS **G**REATLY **O**VERDRAMATIZING **H**EROIC **O**PERATIONS. **P**REFERENCE-ER.

THE LION KING

TAKE HEED! EISNER'S LICENSING INCOME OVERFLOWING NOW. KIDS INFATUATED. NOT GOOD.

ET

ENOUGH TERRESTRIALS.

THE NANNY

TOTAL HEADACHE ENTERTAINMENT.
NAGGING AND NEEDLING,
NUDGING, YENTA-ING.

SiSTERS

SUCH iDiOTiC STORIES. TALENTLESS
ENSEMBLE REALLY SUCKS.

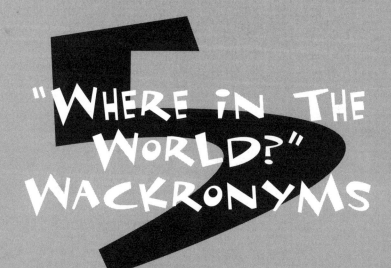

5

"WHERE IN THE WORLD?" WACKRONYMS

BOSTON

BATTLE OVER SPILLED TEA
OLD NEWS.

CALIFORNIA

CITIZENS ALL LIVE IN FEAR OF RUMBLING, NEXT INTERRUPTIVE AFTERSHOCK.

NEW YORK CITY

NEVER ENTER WITHOUT
YOUR OWN REVOLVER KEPT
CLOSE. IF TROUBLE, YELL!

FLORIDA

FEEBLE-LOOKING OLDSTERS. REALLY
INCOMPETENT DRIVERS. AVOID.

A CAVALCADE OF WACKRONYMS

METS

MAKE ERRORS. THEY STINK.

GiRL SCOUTS

GROUP iRRESPONSiBLY RETAiLiNG
LOUSY STALE COOKiES, OTHERWiSE
USELESS TREATS. STOP!

WoMEN

WANT ORGASMS. MEN EQUAL? NOT!

HEARING AiD

Hi. EH? AuDiO REALLY
iNCOMPREHENSiBLE. NO GOOD.
AGAiN? i DUNNO.

CALCULUS

CAN ANYONE LEGITIMATELY CONCEIVE USING LATER? UTTER STUPIDITY.

iNFLUENZA

i NOW FEEL LOUSY, UPSET, EXTREMELY NAUSEOUS. ZERO ADRENALINE.

THUMB

TRAVELING HiTCHHiKER
USUALLY MUST BEG.

CREDIT CARD

CASH RESERVES EMPTY? DISCOVER IS TERRIFIC. CREATIVELY ABUSE REVOLVING DEBT.

PiG

PORK iS GOOD.

COW

CUD? OH WOW.

GOLF

Go Out, Look Foolish.

CAT

CALICOS AIN'T TRAINABLE.

BASEBALL

BORING AMERICAN SPORT
ERADICATED BY A LABOR LOCKOUT.

GiN

GET INTOXICATED NIGHTLY.

MAFIA

MAKE A FORTUNE INSTANTLY—
ASSASSINATE.

DEATH

FOR ATHEISTS:
DON'T EXPECT ANYTHING TO HAPPEN.
FOR BELIEVERS:
DEPART EARTH AND TRAVEL
HEAVENWARD.

AGENT

AMAZINGLY GREEDY.
EXPLOITS NOTEWORTHY TALENT.

FENCE

FRIENDS, ENEMIES, NEIGHBORS
CAN'T EAVESDROP.

GREED

GIMME RICHES. EVERYONE ELSE DIE.

DENTIST

DOCTOR ENJOYS NEEDLING TORTUROUS INCISORS. SINISTER TYRANT!

MIDNIGHT

MY, IT'S DARK NOW.
I'M GOING HOME TOO.

PERSONAL ADS

PEOPLE EXPECTING ROMANCE SEND
OPTIMISTIC NOTES. ALL LIES.
ANOTHER DATELESS SATURDAY.

BLIND DATES

BASICALLY LONELY INDIVIDUALS NEGOTIATE DINNER. DOES ANYONE TRULY EXPECT SUCCESS?

DOG

DUMPS ON GROUND.

HOCKEY

HUNDREDS OF CANADIANS KILLED EVERY YEAR.

SHOE

SMELLS HORRIBLE.
ODOREATERS ESSENTIAL.

KARATE

KICK ASS. RELIEVE ANGER.
TESTICLES ENDANGERED.

MEDiCARE

MONEY'S EVADORATING. DOCTOR
iNSURANCE CAN'T ACTUALLY
RESCUE EVERYONE.

WACKRONYMS

WACKY! AMAZING! CRAZY! KOOKY!
RIOTOUS! OUTRAGEOUS! NOTORIOUS!
YUMMY! MANIACAL! SILLY!

Now that you've read our WACKRONYMS, why not try inventing some of your own? And if you come up with a really great one based on a popular person, place, thing, title or whatever, we'd love to see it. And if we use it in an upcoming edition of WACKRONYMS, we'll credit your creation for the world to see. Send your WACKRONYMS to:

WACKRONYMS
℅ The Literary Group
270 Lafayette Street
New York, New York 10012

or e-mail us at: WACKRONYMS@AOL.COM